The Presidents of the United States 28 – 46 ™ & © 2023 Lina Beijerstam & Markosia Enterprises, Ltd. All Rights Reserved. Reproduction of any part of this work by any means without the written permission of the publisher is expressly forbidden. Published by Markosia Enterprises, PO BOX 3477, Barnet, Hertfordshire, EN5 9HN. FIRST PRINTING, December 2023. Harry Markos, Director.

ISBN 978-1-915860-98-9

www.markosia.com

Introduction

Let us get some knowledge to understand the political system in the United States with a fun and short explanation of the most influential presidents. Starting with numbers 28-46.

Short and important facts from the 28th president of America to 46th.

We first need to know is a short introduction to the country we call today The United States and how it became the United States.

How America became independent

For thousands of years, Native Americans lived on the continent we call North America, the United States. People from Europe, mostly from England, France, Spain, and the Netherlands, colonized North America in the early 1600s to increase wealth and broaden their influence over the world. England had the most dominant presence.

In 1775 the American revolution started, the war for independence from the strong British control over its 13 colonies. April 30th, 1789, George Washington, the commander in chief of the continental army, declared America's victory and became the United States' first president.

George Washington, among others also called the 'founding fathers', helped bring together the U.S constitution documents, including the articles of confederation and declaration of independence.

Book Navigator

TABLE OF CONTENTS

The American Government

The American Presidency

First president

GEORGE WASHINGTON 1789-1797

"99% of failures come from people who make excuses."

An American president in the United States is elected indirectly through the United States Electoral College to a term; each term is 4 years with a limit of two terms.

The American Government

The United States is a representative democracy. This means that citizens elect the US government.

There are 3 branches of the US Government

1. Legislative (makes laws) with its congress, senate and house of representatives
2. Executive with its President (carries out laws), vice president and cabinet
3. Judicial (interprets laws) with its supreme court other federal courts

World War 1
1914–1918

World War I began in 1914 after the assassination of Archduke Franz Ferdinand of Austria. His murder led Europe into a war that lasted until 1918. During the conflict, Germany, Austria-Hungary, Bulgaria, and the Ottoman Empire (the Central Powers) fought against Great Britain, France, Russia, Italy, Romania, Japan, and the United States (the Allied Powers).

Why did the war start?
The short explanation is– militarism, alliances, imperialism, and nationalism conflicts between the countries. Each of these reasons is a few to be mentioned as some of the main causes of World War One.

Leaders:
The Allies leaders were Georges Clemenceau(France), David Lloyd George (The Great Britain), Nicolas 11 (Russia), Emperor Taishō(Japan), Woodrow Wilson (United States), Vittorio Emanuele (Italy), Ferdinand I(Romania)The Central Powers were Wilhelm II (Germany), Franz Joseph (Austria-Hungary),Vasil Radoslavov(Bulgaria), Enver Pasha (Ottoman Empire).

World War 2
1939–1945

World War 2 began in 1939 when the dictator of Germany, Adolf Hitler invaded Poland. During the conflict, Great Britain, The United States, and the Soviet Union (the Allied Powers) fought against Germany, Japan, and Italy (the Axis Powers).

Why did the war start?
The short explanation is– The German desire for revenge after its impact on the economy after WW1- (The Treaty of Versailles), Economic downturns In Europe, civil, political, and international disturbance, the threat of Nazi ideology and Lebensraum, the forming of alliances and the rise of extremism. After WW1, Europe changed with political players on the extreme right and left. Each of these reasons is just a few mentioned as some of the main causes of World War 2.

Leaders:
The Axis leaders were Adolf Hitler (Germany), Benito Mussolini (Italy), and Emperor Hirohito (Japan). The Allies were Franklin Roosevelt (the United States), Winston Churchill (Great Britain), and Joseph Stalin (the Soviet Union).

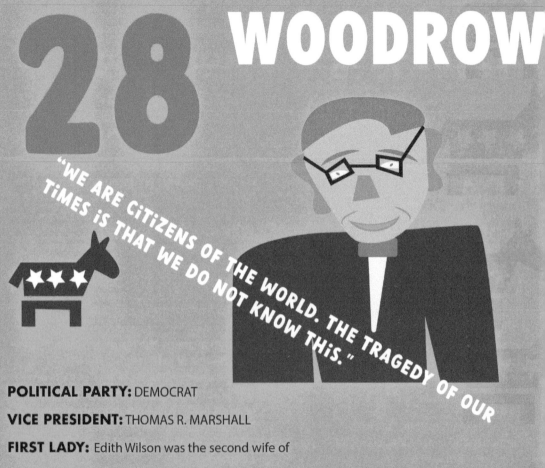

28 WOODROW

"WE ARE CITIZENS OF THE WORLD. THE TRAGEDY OF OUR TIMES IS THAT WE DO NOT KNOW THIS."

POLITICAL PARTY: DEMOCRAT

VICE PRESIDENT: THOMAS R. MARSHALL

FIRST LADY: Edith Wilson was the second wife of President Woodrow Wilson and served as the First Lady of the United States from 1915 to 1921.

WILSON

Fact: Woodrow Wilson became the 28th President of America in 1913. He was 56 years old and served for 8 years until 1921; he intended to run for a 3rd. Term but suffered from a stroke that led to his death. On May 7, 1915, a cruise ship with American citizens on board got sunk by a German submarine, for this, among other political and economic reasons, Wilson led the U.S into World War 1.

Wilson was the first American president to cross the Atlantic Ocean because of the war and establish a peace treaty he accomplished in 1918, the treaty of Versailles, signed by the Allied. Among other important points, The Treaty of Versailles held Germany responsible for starting the war. Wilson did not join The League of Nations (an international peacekeeping organization meant to keep the peace in the aftermath of World War I.

During his first term as president, Woodrow Wilson focused on three types of reform: tariff reform, banking reform, and business reform.

He accomplished to pass: The Federal Reserve Act (the central banking system of the United States), the Federal Trade Commission Act(stopping unfair, deceptive, or fraudulent practices in the marketplace), the Clayton Antitrust Act (to stop anti competitive practice by prohibiting certain types of behaviors)the Federal Farm Loan Act(help small farmers and ranchers by making it easier for farmers to secure loans), and an income tax.

One other major accomplishment during Wilsons's presidency was voting rights for women.

DID YOU KNOW?

Wilson issued a declaration of a national Mother's Day and that it would occur on the second Sunday of May every year

He was awarded the Nobel Peace Prize in 1920 for his contributions toward ending the war

He was the first president to visit Europe while still in office

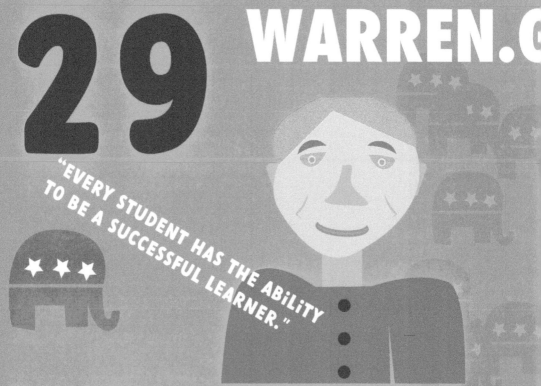

"EVERY STUDENT HAS THE ABiLiTY TO BE A SUCCESSFUL LEARNER."

POLITICAL PARTY: REPUBLICAN

VICE PRESIDENT: Calvin Coolidge 1921-1923

FIRST LADY: Florence Mabel Harding was the wife of President Warren G. Harding and served as the First Lady of the United States from 1921 to 1923.

HARDING

Fact: Warren G. Harding became the 29th President of the United States in 1921. He was 55 years old and served for 2 years until his death, supposedly caused by a heart attack on a trip to Alaska in 1923.

Harding's election was a landslide, he promised the people to, as he quoted, "return to normalcy" after World War 1 harsh impacts on the country. Harding's approach was based on conservative republican agenda, pro-business with reduced taxes, mostly for the wealthy and large corporations. Immigration became limited, and high tariffs were portrayed.

The Teapot Dome scandal, the administration of United States with Warren as president, was a huge bribery scandal, Secretary of the Interior Albert Bacon Fall had leased Navy petroleum reserves at Teapot Dome in Wyoming, as well as two locations in California, to private oil companies at low rates without competitive bidding.

DID YOU KNOW?

He was the first president to talk on the radio

Harding was the first president elected after women had received the right to vote per the 19th amendment

He was the first president to visit Alaska and Canada

30

CALVIN

> "WE CANNOT DO EVERYTHING AT ONCE, BUT WE CAN DO SOMETHING AT ONCE."

POLITICAL PARTY: REPUBLICAN

VICE PRESIDENT: Charles G. Dawes 1925–1929

FIRST LADY: Grace Anna Coolidge was the wife of

Calvin Coolidge and served as the first lady

of the United States from 1923 to 1929.

COOLIDGE

Fact: Calvin Coolidge became the 30th President of America in 1923; he was 51 years old and served for 6 years. Coolidge served as Vice President during Harding's presidency and won the election in a three-way contest.

During Coolidge's presidency, he was known for developing the Dawes plan, a plan made to resolve the European financial consequences of World War 1. The Kellogg-Briand pact signed by the United Kingdom, Japan, France, Italy, and Germany as an international agreement promised not to use war to resolve "disputes or conflicts of whatever nature or of whatever origin they may be, which may arise among them."

Other achievements in foreign policy were the Washington Naval Conference, where the world's major naval powers signed a contract on a naval disarmament program.

In 1928, Coolidge announced to America that he would not run for re-election.

DID YOU KNOW?

Coolidge wasn't very talkative

Coolidge was born on the fourth of July

His nickname "silent Cal" suggests, he's also known for being a man of few words. many historians refer to him as "the best president you've probably never heard of"

31

"WORDS WiTHOUT ACTiONS ARE THE ASSASSiNS OF iDEALiSM"

POLITICAL PARTY: REPUBLICAN

VICE PRESIDENT: Charles Curtis 1929-1933

FIRST LADY: Lou Hoover was the wife of President

Herbert Hoover and served as the First Lady

of the United States from 1929 to 1933.

12

HOOVER

Fact: Herbert Hoover became the 31st President of America in 1929. He was 54 years old and served for 4 years. He won the election promising to ensure prosperity to the people, "We in America today are nearer to the final triumph over poverty than ever before in the history of any land."

Hoover is mostly known for being the president during the stock market crash that occurred just 7 months after he took office in 1929, putting America into the great depression. During this time, Unemployment rates rose from 3% to 23 %, businesses and banks were forced to close because of bankruptcy. It went so bad that many people had to wait in lines for food and live-in towns with horrible conditions.

Hoover's solution met a lot of critics. He designed programs to stimulate the economy based on his conservative political philosophy. In the end, Hoover became the one to blame for The Great Depression and was badly defeated in the election 1932.

Achievements in the foreign policy during Hoover's presidency were among improved relations with Latin America, keeping America out of the war in Asia and success in achieving disarmament the large naval powers.

DID YOU KNOW?

Hoover was viewed as insensitive toward the suffering of millions of U.S. citizens

He won the presidency in his first-ever election campaign

Before Hoover became president, he starred in the first television broadcast in American history

32 FRANKLIN.D

"THERE ARE MANY WAYS OF GOiNG FORWARD, BUT ONLY ONE WAY OF STANDiNG STiLL."

POLITICAL PARTY: DEMOCRAT

VICE PRESIDENT: John Nance Garner (1933–1941)

Henry A. Wallace (1941–1945) Harry S. Truman (1945)

FIRST LADY: Anna Eleanor Roosevelt was the wife of

President Franklin D Roosevelt and served as the First

Lady of the United States from 1933-1945.

ROOSEVELT 1933-1945

Fact: Franklin D Roosevelt became the 32nd President of America in 1933; he was 51 years old and the only president to be elected to the office 4 times, 12 years.

During Roosevelt's times, he led America through two of the greatest crises in history in the 20th century: The Great Depression and World War 2. Roosevelt created the New Deal for the American people, a series of reforms and programs whose aim was to expand the Government's role in the economy, giving the power to regulate areas of commerce, such as banking, agriculture, and housing, which hadn't been regulated before. He also created programs allowing social security and welfare aid for the poor.

During the War in Europe 1939, Roosevelt provided the allies Great Britain and France, allowing congress to sell military support. On December 8, 1941, the Japanese attacked the naval base in Pearl Harbor. This was a catalys at or for America to enter the War; World War 2 was established.

Roosevelt started to communicate along with the Allied countries combating the Axis. He frequently met with Britain's leader Winston Churchill on how to end the war in peaceful manners and to establish friendly relations with the Soviet Union and its leader Joseph Stalin.

DID YOU KNOW?

Roosevelt is considered one of the best presidents in U.S. history

He helped lay the foundation for future peace by working to build an international peace organization that would become known as the United Nations

Roosevelt was the first President to win a Nobel Peace Prize

33

HARRY.S

"iT iS iGNORANCE THAT CAUSES MOST MiSTAKES."

POLITICAL PARTY: DEMOCRAT

VICE PRESIDENT: None (1945-1949) Alben W. Barkley (1949-1953)

FIRST LADY: Elizabeth Virginia Truman was the wife of President Harry S. Truman and served as the First Lady of the United States from 1945 to 1953.

TRUMAN

Fact: Harry S Truman became the 33rd President of America in 1945, he was 60 years old and served for 8 years. Truman is known for making some of the most crucial decisions in history; the atomic bombs to defeat the war against Japan, destroyed the cities Hiroshima and Nagasaki and killed between 129,000 and 226,000 people. He helped rebuild postwar Europe and worked to prevent communist influence. Truman also led America into the Korean War (1950-1953)

The Korean War was against communism; American troops entered the war on South Korea's behalf. The invasion is known as the first military action of the cold war, where the communist Soviet-backed north attacked the south.

During Truman's time in office, other great accomplishments were among the Establishment of the NSC, the CIA, and the NSA, intelligence to protect the national security systems and help with foreign policies.

North Atlantic Treaty Organization (NATO) Formation, he established together with Canada and a few European countries, organization aimed to form security structures of democratic ideals and control the Soviet expansion.

DID YOU KNOW?

He served as the vice president for just 82 days

Truman pushed for universal health insurance

He almost doubled the minimum wage

34 DWIGHT.D

"MOTiVATiON iS THE ART OF GETTiNG PEOPLE TO DO WHAT YOU WANT THEM TO DO BECAUSE THEY WANT TO DO iT."

POLITICAL PARTY: REPUBLICAN

VICE PRESIDENT: Richard Nixon (1953-1961)

FIRST LADY: Mary Geneva Eisenhower was the wife of

President Dwight D. Eisenhower and served as the First Lady

of the United States from 1953 to 1961.

EISENHOWER 1953-1961

Fact: D Dwight D. Eisenhower became the 34th President of America in 1953, he was 63 years old and served for 8 years. Before running as the candidate for the Republican party, Eisenhower had a background in a successful military career. He campaigned with promises to defeat communism, Corruption and the conflict in Korea.

During his presidency, Eisenhower managed the Cold War-era tensions with the Soviet Union and obtained a truce in Korea in 1953. He also set up anti-communist operations by the CIA around the world. In 1956, he signed the Federal-Aid Highway Act and gave birth to America's interstate highway system.

Eisenhower became the founder of NASA in 1958. The space race was between the Soviet Union and The United States.

The Soviets beat America in launching the first satellite, Sputnik 1, 1957, 4th of October. In response, Eisenhower created the National Aeronautics and space administration (NASA), a civilian space agency responsible for the space program and aeronautics and aerospace research.

DID YOU KNOW?

Eisenhower opposed using nuclear weapons on Japan

Alaska and Hawaii became states under his watch

Eisenhower became the first president constitutionally prevented from seeking a third term

35

JOHN.F

"ASK NOT WHAT YOUR COUNTRY CAN DO FOR YOU – ASK WHAT YOU CAN DO FOR YOUR COUNTRY."

POLITICAL PARTY: DEMOCRAT

VICE PRESIDENT: Lyndon B. Johnson (1961-1963)

FIRST LADY: Jacqueline Lee "Jackie" Kennedy Onassis was

the wife of President John F. Kennedy. And served as the

First Lady of the United States from 1961-1963.

KENNEDY

Fact: John F. Kennedy became the 35th President of America in 1961. He was 43 years old and served for 2 years until his assassination in 1963.

During the time Kennedy campaigned for president, the Cold War tension was rising between America and the Soviet Union. Americans were afraid that the communist countries would rise beyond science and technology. Cuba became a close ally of the Soviet Union. November 8th, 1960, John Kennedy won the election in one of the closest elections in American history.

Kennedy was considered a great president; however, there were many failures during his presidency. In 1961, the Bay of pigs, with its goals to overthrow the Government of the communist leader Fidel Castor failed. He also met with the Soviet premier Nikita Khrushchev in Vienna, but the meeting did not end in any resolution to the long-standing conflict over the status of Berlin. The city was divided after World War 1, Soviet-supported East Berlin, and Western allies-supported West Berlin.

Accomplishments during Kennedy's presidency were, among others, an aggressive space program. 1962 America successfully sent John Glenn into space, competing with the Soviets, who 1961 launched the first man, Yuri Gargain, into orbit. He created the Peace Corps, a program to help underdeveloped nations with farming, education, health care and construction. He was the creator of the Equal Pay Act, with its purpose to eliminate wage inequality based on sex.

On November 22, 1963, John.F. Kennedy was assassinated during a campaign visit at 12:30, in Dallas while riding a motorcade. He was 46 years old.

DID YOU KNOW?

J. F. Kennedy grew up in a wealthy and powerful political family

He remains the youngest elected president in US history

J. F. Kennedy gave one of the most famous inaugural speeches in history

"YOU AREN'T LEARNING ANYTHING WHEN YOU'RE TALKING."

POLITICAL PARTY: DEMOCRAT

VICE PRESIDENT: Hubert Humphrey (1965-1969)

FIRST LADY: Claudia Alta "Lady Bird" Johnson was the wife of Lyndon B. Johnson. And served as the First Lady of the United States from 1963 to 1969.

JOHNSON

Fact: Lyndon B. Johnson became the 36th President of America in 1963, he was 55 years old and served for 6 years.

Johnson was the Vice President during J. F Kennedy's presidency, shortly after his death, Johnson became the president of America. During his first years, Johnson wanted to obtain the visions of J.F Kennedy. He urged the Nation to "build a great society". By introducing the great society programs, everyone would be treated equally and have equal opportunity. Key points: War on poverty, Medicare and Medicaid, Head start and Education reform, Urban renewal, support for arts and humanities.

As a result, more than 60 education bills got passed during his presidency. In 1965, the Medicare Amendment to the social security act was introduced, allowing millions of elderly people proper medical care. The voting rights Act of 1965 was one of his major introductions, making it more eligible for people of any color to vote.

Johnson downfall was the handling of the Vietnam War. During his presidency, America got more involved as the war escalated, and his popularity began to diminish.

Lyndon B Johnson decided not to run for a second full term in the 1968 presidential election. Republican Richard Nixon succeeded him. Johnson died of a heart attack at age 64 on January 22, 1973, at his ranch.

DID YOU KNOW?

Johnson's wife, lady bird, was key to his success

The war in Vietnam lead Johnson into depression and brought his presidency to an end

He appointed the first African American to the Supreme Court, Thurgood Marshall

37

RICHARD

"WHAT A STRANGE CREATURE MAN IS THAT HE FOULS HIS OWN NEST."

POLITICAL PARTY: REPUBLICAN

VICE PRESIDENT: Spiro Agnew (1969–1973),

Gerald Ford (1973–1974)

FIRST LADY: Patricia Ryan Nixon was the wife of

Richard Nixon and served as the First Lady

of the United States from 1969 to 1974.

NIXON

Fact: Richard Nixon became the 37th President of America in 1969. He was 56 years old and served for 5 years until his resignation.

Before Richard Nixon won the presidential election in 1969, he had been the Vice president for two terms under Dwight Eisenhower. In 1960, Nixon lost the run for the presidency in a close battle with Democrat John F. Kennedy. He ran for the White House again and won in 1968.

Nixon became president during a time when the American people's behavior was about to change, it was a period of revolt. The Americans were divided over the Vietnam War, and protests and riots became common. Women and black Americans started protesting for equal rights; change was needed.

During Nixon's Presidency his achievements included matters such as repairing diplomatic ties with communist China and The Soviet Union. In 1972, Nixon visited the People's Republic of China and became the United States' first president to do. He withdrew American troops from the war in Vietnam, with the Paris Peace Accords, 1973. On July 21, 1969, Neil Armstrong became the first man to walk on the moon, one of the biggest events in the world that Nixon's cabinet made sure to happen. Nixon also enforced several groundbreaking environmental measures.

June 17, 1972, known as the Watergate Scandal, police arrested five men breaking into the Democratic Party headquarters in the Watergate Buildings in Washington D.C. The men worked for Nixon, collecting evidence for Nixon's re-election campaign in, which he denied. August 9, 1974, Richard Nixon resigned from office. Nixon's involvement in Watergate deepened American skepticism about Government.

DID YOU KNOW?

Nixon's funding for his first political campaign came after playing poker while serving in the U.S Navy

Richard Nixon almost became an FBI agent in the 1930s

Richard Nixon wanted the secret service to wear uniforms

38

GERALD

"TELL THE TRUTH, WORK HARD, AND COME TO DINNER ON TIME."

POLITICAL PARTY: REPUBLICAN

VICE PRESIDENT: Nelson Rockefeller (1974-1977)

FIRST LADY: Elizabeth Anne Ford was the wife of Gerald Ford and served as the First Lady of the United States from 1974 to 1977.

FORD

Fact: Gerald Ford became the 38th President of America in 1974; he was 61years old and served for 4 years until he lost the election in 1976 to Democrat Jimmy Carter.

Gerald R. Ford had served as Vice President for only 9 months until he became the President of America. He became the only president without winning a general election. Ford had to face inflation, a depressed economy, and trying to certify world peace.

During his presidency, Ford continued Nixon's effort on foreign relations. He established new treaties with The Soviets and brokered a temporary truce in the Middle East. However, during Ford's time at the office, the country entered a recession with high inflation.

Ford did some major improvements to America's economy; more than half during his presidency the inflation rate decreased. He did this by increasing spending and cutting taxes targeted at low- and moderate-income families. His policies also stimulated the creation of more jobs, and the unemployment rate fell drastically.

Ford left the office and ended his political career after being defeated. He died in 2006 at the age of 96, the longest living President in history.

DID YOU KNOW?

His birth name wasn't Gerald R. Ford. Ford was born as Leslie Lynch King Jr

Ford wasn't elected to the office of vice president or president

Ford stood by his decision to pardon Nixon even though it might have cost him re-election

"YOU CAN DO WHAT YOU HAVE TO DO, AND SOMETIMES YOU CAN DO IT EVEN BETTER THAN YOU THINK YOU CAN."

POLITICAL PARTY: DEMOCRAT

VICE PRESIDENT: Walter Mondale (1977-1991)

FIRST LADY: Eleanor Rosalynn Carter was the wife of

Jimmy Carter and served as the First Lady

of the United States from 1977 to 1981.

CARTER

Fact: Jimmy Carter became the 39th President of America in 1977, he was 52 years old and served for 4 years.

Carter's Presidency was an effect of the aftermath of the Watergate scandal. It had created doubt in people regarding the leadership of the Government. He approached himself as an outsider to Washington D.C, a man with principles who could restore faith in the American people for their leaders. During Carters time at the office, he failed to deal with the problems that the Americans were hit hard of, rising energy costs, inflation, and world tensions.

However, he and his administration accomplished the Panama Canal treaties recognized Panama as the territorial dominant in the Canal Zone and the United States the right to continue operating the canal. The Camp David Accords- a historical first treaty between Israel and its Arab neighbors. The Agreement was signed between Egypt and Israel. The SALT II treaty with the Soviet- reduced the manufacture of nuclear weapons. The administration also established the US diplomatic relations with the People's Republic of China. Other accomplishments were the new energy program and new major educational programs.

DID YOU KNOW?

Carter won the Nobel Peace Prize in 2002 for his efforts in human rights and peace

In response to the Soviet Union invading Afghanistan, he had the U.S. boycott the 1980 Summer Olympics

Carter founded the Carter Center, preventing disease issues globally and fighting for human rights

"TRUST, BUT VERiFY."

POLITICAL PARTY: REPUBLICAN

VICE PRESIDENT: George H.W. Bush (1981-1989)

FIRST LADY: Nancy Davis Reagan was the wife of

Ronald Reagan and served as the First Lady

of the United States from 1981 to 1989.

DID YOU KNOW?

Reagan started out in life as a Democrat and supported the New Deal efforts of President
Franklin D. Roosevelt

Reagan was an FBI informant. increasingly involved
in politics in the 40s

There have been at least 10 statues erected
in his honor

REAGAN

Fact: Ronald Reagan became the 40th President of America in 1981, he was 69 years old and served for 8 years.

Before his presidency, Reagan worked as a Hollywood actor and as the Republican governor of California. Reagan is known for being the "Great Communicator" and spoke well to the public. In his inaugural address, he quoted "In this present crisis, Government is not the solution to our problems; Government is the problem.

During Reagan's time at the office, he and his administration were challenged with an America that has experienced high inflation, unemployment, rising gas prices and the cold war.

In order to make people feel confident again, Reaganomics was introduced in order to get inflation down and employment up. This meant cutting taxes and increasing defense spending. As a result, the inflation rate went from 13,5% in his first year of office to 4% when he left.

America for many years had been in a Cold War with the Soviet. Both had the atomic bomb and were considered the world's two Superpowers. One of his administration initiatives was the Reagan Doctrine, aid provided to anti-communist movements in Africa, and SDI; development of space-based weapons to protect America from attacks by Soviet nuclear missiles.

Reagan accomplished a diplomatic relationship with Mikhail Gorbachev, the leader of the Soviet.1987, the Soviet and America signed a historic agreement to eliminate nuclear missiles; the same year Reagan also challenged Gorbachev to tear down the Berlin war.

Leaving the White House in, 1989 Ronald returned to California with his wife. He later announced to the public he was diagnosed with Alzheimer's. Reagan died in his home at the age of 93 in 2004.

41

GEORGE.

"I HAVE OPINIONS OF MY OWN, STRONG OPINIONS, BUT I DON'T ALWAYS AGREE WITH THEM."

POLITICAL PARTY: REPUBLICAN

VICE PRESIDENT: Dan Quayle Bush (1989-1993)

FIRST LADY: Barbara Pierce Bush was the wife of George H.W Bush and served as the First Lady of the United States from 1989 to 1993.

DID YOU KNOW?

In 1993 H.W Bush was knighted by Queen Elizabeth II. He was the third American president to receive the honorary knighthood

After graduating from Yale, he went out on his own and entered the oil business

H.W Bush came from a political family

HW BUSH

1989-1993

Fact: George H.W Bush became the 41st President of America in 1989. He was 64 years old and served for 4 years.

Before H.W Bush became president, he was the Vice president during Ronald Reagan's time. He was also a war veteran, having served in the U.S Navy during World War 11.

Facing a changing world where the 40-year lasting Cold War finally came to an end and with the communist empire breaking up forming new nations, Bush greeted the march of Democracy and insisted on keeping the U.S policy toward the new group of the new nations.

During his presidency, he sent the American troops into Panama, where the dictator Noriega had seized power threatening the security of the canal and the Americans living there. Bush's ultimate test came when in 1990, the dictator of Iraq, Saddam Hussein invaded the small, rich oil country Kuwait, also known as The Gulf War, Bush sent American troops to Kuwait to help defeat Hussein, the 100-

hour land battle, "Operation Desert Storm" overpowered Iraq's army.

Bush managed to sign the NAFTA, North American Free Trade Agreement, between the United States, Canada, and Mexico. With its purpose to eliminate harsh tariffs between the nations, restricted patents, copyrights, and trademarks.

The American Economy began to struggle near the end of Bush's term. Despite popularity from the military and diplomatic triumph, Bush did not manage to keep his popularity and lost his bid for re-election to Democrat Bill Clinton.

H.W Bush retired after leaving his post as the American President and moved to Texas with his wife, Barbara Pierce Bush. He died on November 30, 2018.

42

"CHARACTER iS A JOURNEY, NOT A DESTiNATiON."

POLITICAL PARTY: DEMOCRAT

VICE PRESIDENT: Al Gore (1993-2001)

FIRST LADY: Hillary Clinton was the wife of Bill Clinton

and served as the First Lady of the United States

from 1993 to 2001.

Fact: Bill Clinton became the 42nd President of America in 1991, he was 64 years old and served for 8 years.

Before beating George H.W Bush in the presidential election, no one thought Clinton had a chance to win the presidency. He entered the office at a time when the American economy was struggling. Clinton and his administration's greatest accomplishments were leading the nation to a generation with more peace and economic well-being at any time in history, the lowest unemployment rate in modern times, the lowest inflation in 30 years and the highest homeownership in history. Moreover, Clinton achieved a budget excess and introduced the first balanced budget.

Achievements in foreign policy- Clinton negotiated the Oslo Accord between Israel and the Palestine Liberation Organization. Its main purpose is to negate violence in the Israeli-Palestine conflict. He kept forces from warn-torn Bosnia and bombed Iraq when Saddam Hussein stopped the United Nations inspections for evidence of nuclear.

He advocated for open international trade, drug trafficking and an expanded NATO.

In 1998, Clinton was accused of having an affair with Monica Lewinsky, which he denied. Lying in court is a perjury offense, so the House of Representatives voted to impeach Clinton. However, the Senate didn't agree, and he was allowed to stay in office.

After leaving office in 2000, Clinton kept himself busy writing books and giving speeches.

DID YOU KNOW?

He was the first two term president from the Democratic Party since Franklin D. Roosevelt

Clinton's wife, Hillary Rodham Clinton, has been a U.S. Senator from New York and U.S. Secretary of State. And a presidential candidate in 2016

He was the second US president to be impeached. The first was Andrew Johnson in 1868

43 GEORGE.W

"EVERYWHERE THAT FREEDOM STiRS, LET TYRANTS FEAR. "

POLITICAL PARTY: REPUBLICAN

VICE PRESIDENT: Dick Cheney (2001-2009)

FIRST LADY: Laura Lane Welch Bush was the wife of

George Bush and served as the First Lady

of the United States from 2001 to 2009.

DID YOU KNOW?

He has been one of the most popular and one of the lea
popular presidents in the US history

Bush speaking about the 9/11 attacks, has said, "I beca
something I did not want to be: a wartime president"

He pushed through legislation that helped Texas become
the number one producer of wind-powered energy in
America

Fact: George Bush became the 43rd President of America in 2001, he was 54 years old and served for 8 years.

George W. Bush is the son of past president George H.W Bush. He won the presidency over Al Gore in one of the closest of the time, the most controversial elections in American history.

Short after Bush took office, the American economy began to struggle. "The dot-com" bubble (a stock market bubble caused by excessive speculation of Internet-related companies) occurred, many people lost their jobs and investments during this period.

September 11, 2001, an airborne terrorist attack on the World Trade Center, the Pentagon and the flight aimed to the White House, in which nearly 3,000 Americans were killed, made Bush "face one of the greatest challenges of any president since Abraham Lincoln" as his father declared. A month after the attack, America invaded Afghanistan to overthrow the Taliban government.
The Government was suspected of hiding Osama Bin Laden, the leader of Al-Qaeda. While the Government was overthrown, Bin Laden was not captured until many years later.

The Bush administration blamed Saddam Hussein, the dictator of Iraq, for its attack and suspected that Iraq had weapons of mass destruction. Iraq refused to comply with inspections of these allegations, and the Iraq War began. America invaded Iraq; although the initial invasion was successful, helping Iraq to rebuild the country and establish a new government became a very difficult task.

During his first term at the office, Bush achievements were among tax-cut bills, Medicare prescription, drug program for seniors, the No Child Left Behind Act (to hold schools accountable for student learning and achievement). However, the economy began to struggle, unemployment rose, and Bush's popularity lost degraded slowly. At the time he left office, his endorsement ratings reached an all-time low.

44

BARACK

"WE ARE THE CHANGE WE HAVE BEEN WAITING FOR."

POLITICAL PARTY: DEMOCRAT

VICE PRESIDENT: Joe Biden (2009-2017)

FIRST LADY: Michelle Lavaughn Robinson Obama was the wife of Barack Obama and served as the First Lady of the United States from 2009 to 2017.

DID YOU KNOW?

He lived in Indonesia from age 6 to 10 with his mother and stepfather

As a state senator, Obama sponsored and led the passage of Illinois' first racial-profiling law, which requires the police to videotape homicide interrogations

In 2008 and 2012, he became the "Person of the Year" in the Time magazine

OBAMA

Fact: Barack Obama became the 44th President of America in 2009, he was 47years old and served for 8 years.

Obama became the first African American to hold office; he won the election with a landslide defeating John McCain.

Many challenges were to face when Obama entered office – an economic collapse, wars in Iraq and Afghanistan and the threat of terrorism. Obama wanted to reintroduce America's status globally and bring back the economy to the people. During his first team, he signed three bills. A bill to stimulate the economy, legislation, making health care more affordable and accessible, also referred to as "Obamacare" and legislation changing the nation's financial institutions.

Other achievements during his presidency included the fair pay act for women, financial reform legislation, efforts for consumer protection.

As for the foreign policy, the Middle East continued a key challenge; he managed the killing of Osama bin Laden and succeeded in a nuclear program agreement with Iran. Obama also established diplomatic relations with Cuba and became the first sitting president to visit Cuba since 1928. When Obama became the President, the Iraq and Afghanistan Wars were ongoing, although he successfully ended the Iraq war in 2011. The Afghanistan War did proceed during his presidency. The Obama administration also signed a climate change agreement with 195 other nations to reduce greenhouse gases emissions and slow down global warming.

The economy during his time in office has remained controversial. Unemployment peaked at 10% in 2009. However, it is estimated that over 11 million jobs were created during his two terms. Obama pushed for higher taxes, a larger federal government and stimulus plans. The GDP overall economy showed slow improvements.

Obama left the office and handed over the job to Donald Trump. Obama's post-presidential life is included globetrotting and book-writing.

45

DONALD

"AS LONG AS YOU'RE GOING TO BE THINKING ANYWAY, THINK BIG."

POLITICAL PARTY: REPUBLICAN

VICE PRESIDENT: Mike Pence (2017-2021)

FIRST LADY: Melania Trump was the wife of Donald Trump and served as the First Lady of the United States from 2009 to 2017.

DID YOU KNOW?

Trump has a star on the Hollywood Walk of Fame

During Trump's presidency, many have characterized his comments and actions as racially abusive or racist

He is the only U.S. President who does not have previous military or governmental experience

TRUMP

Fact: Donald Trump became the 45th President of America in 2017, he was 71 years old and served for 4 years.

Before Donald John Trump won the election in 2017, he was known as an American real-estate developer, businessman, and media personality. During the election in 2016, Trumps opponent was Hillary Clinton, a former secretary of state and wife to former U.S. president Bill Clinton.

Trump's campaign slogan was "Make America Great again". During his presidency, he ordered a travel ban on citizens from several Muslim-majority countries, proposed tax cuts, repealed the Affordable Care Act, appointed more than 200 federal judges, including three, to the supreme court. As for the foreign policy, he followed an agenda based on the quote "America First". He renegotiated the North American Free Trade Agreement to the United States-Mexico-Canada agreement; he withdrew the U.S from the Trans-Pacific Partnership, the Paris Agreement on climate change and the Iran Nuclear deal. Moreover, the relations with China encouraged a trade war and imposed tariffs for imports from China. With North Korea, he met with the leader and county's dictator, Kim Jong-Un, 3 times without progress on denuclearization.

Other accomplishments during Trump's Presidency were the Abraham accords. With its purpose is to create more opportunities for establishing peace, prosperity, and stability in the Middle East. As an outcome, The Arab nations agreed to normalize relations with Israel.

Trump was accused of having Russian to help him win the 2016 election. He was also one of the presidents impeached over allegations that he sought help from Ukraine to boost his chance of re-election. However, a majority of senators cleared him on two charges. In 2020, the COVID-19 pandemic occurred, and there has been a lot of controversy about the handling of the pandemic.

Trump lost his bid for office in 2020 to previous President Joe Biden.

46

"FAILURE AT SOME POINT IN YOUR LIFE IS INEVITABLE, BUT GIVING UP IS UNFORGIVABLE."

POLITICAL PARTY: DEMOCRAT

VICE PRESIDENT: Kamala Harris (2021-)

FIRST LADY: Jill Tracy Jacobs Biden is the wife of Joe Biden and serves as the First Lady of the United States.

DID YOU KNOW?

Joe Biden is the oldest person elected president

Joe Biden had a childhood stutter, and he has been open about his struggles with it

In 1972, just days before Christmas, Bidens wife and daughter were killed in a car accident, his two sons were seriously injured. He was sworn into the Senate at his sons hospital bedside.

BIDEN

Fact: Fact: Joe Biden became the 46th President of America in 2021 he was 78 years of age and is the current president.

When Joe Biden was elected to the office of President of the United States in the 2020 presidential election, he was 78 years old. This makes him one of the oldest individuals to assume the presidency in American history.

Before his entering to the office, Joe Biden's journey was marked by dedication and public service. He had long been a prominent figure in American politics, serving as a U.S. Senator for Delaware and later as Vice President under President Barack Obama. Joe Biden's long and distinguished career in politics prepared him for the responsibilities of the Oval Office.

In 2020, he stood as the Democratic Party's nominee, facing the incumbent President Donald Trump. The electoral contest was one of the most closely watched in recent memory. Despite the odds, Joe Biden secured the presidency, marking a turning point in American history.

As President, Joe Biden came to be known for his commitment to unity, climate change, healthcare, and a renewed focus on international diplomacy. His administration set out to address pressing issues such as climate change and the ongoing COVID-19 pandemic.

Biden sought to strengthen America's relationships with allies around the world and aimed to restore faith in the country's democratic institutions.

Election Day in the United States of America is the Tuesday following the first Monday in November. It can fall on or between November 2 and November 8. It is the day when popular ballots are held to select public officials. These include national, state, and local government representatives at all levels up to the president.

Who Can Vote?

You can vote in U.S. federal, state, and local elections if you:

Are a U.S. citizen

Meet your state's residency requirements

Are 18 years old on or before Election Day, In almost every state, you can register to vote before you turn 18 if you will be 18 by Election Day.

Are registered to vote by your state's voter registration deadline. North Dakota does not require voter registration.

DID YOU KNOW?

There are three requirements to be president, according to Article II, Section 1, Clause 5 of the U.S. Constitution:

- Must be at least 35 years old
- Have lived in the United States at least 14 years
- Be a natural-born citizen

Three presidents have died in office since 1913:
Warren Harding (heart attack)
Franklin D. Roosevelt (cerebral hemorrhage)
John F. Kennedy (assassination)

Milton Keynes UK
Ingram Content Group UK Ltd.
UKHW050446070224
437285UK00005B/8